BROADCASTERS

CAREERS

William Russell

The Rourke Press, Inc.
Vero Beach, Florida 32964

Edited by Sandra A. Robinson

PHOTO CREDITS
All photos © Lynn M. Stone, except page 8, courtesy KOAA-TV,
Colorado Springs-Pueblo, CO

ACKNOWLEDGMENTS
The author thanks the following organizations for assistance in the
preparation of this book: Connecticut Public Television and Radio
(CPTV) and their Hartford studios; Connecticut School of
Broadcasting, Lombard, IL; KOAA-TV, Colorado Springs-Pueblo,
CO; WKKD-AM and FM, Aurora, IL

Library of Congress Cataloging-in-Publication Data

Russell, William, 1942-
  Broadcasters / by William Russell.
  p. cm. — (Careers)
  Includes index.
  ISBN 1-57103-054-9
  1. Broadcasting—Vocational guidance—Juvenile literature.
[1. Broadcasting—Vocational guidance. 2. Radio broadcasting—
Vocational guidance. 3. Television broadcasting—Vocational
guidance. 4. Vocational guidance.]
I. Title. II. Series: Russell, William, 1942-   Careers.
PN1990.85.R88 1994
791.45'0293—dc20   93-44982
                                      CIP
Printed in the USA   AC

TABLE OF CONTENTS

BROADCASTERS

Broadcasters are people who work as radio and television announcers. Their job, called broadcasting, is to speak to audiences who listen to news, music, sports and information programs.

Broadcasters speak into an instrument called a **microphone,** or "mike." Their words are then broadcast, or transmitted, by the radio or television station to listeners and viewers.

A radio broadcaster hits the switch that will send music over the air

WHAT BROADCASTERS DO

Some broadcasters tell listeners about current events in the news. Other broadcasters talk about weather, traffic, sports, music and other topics.

Talk show broadcasters discuss many different subjects with guests.

Play-by-play sports broadcasters attend sporting events and describe each play of the game as they watch. Their broadcasts help listeners imagine that they, too, are there.

Broadcasters at sporting events, like this minor league baseball game, broadcast play-by-play accounts of the game

KEEPING UP WITH THE WORLD

Broadcasters have more to do than just speak through the microphone. They may spend several hours each day preparing for a broadcast by learning more about the subjects they will discuss. Broadcasters read newspapers and call people to get more information.

Talk show broadcasters have to learn about their guests before they can ask good questions.

Broadcasters help listeners know what is happening in the world around them.

Carefully prepared for his program, a broadcaster goes "live" before the TV camera

WHERE BROADCASTERS WORK

A broadcaster usually works in the broadcasting studio of a radio or TV station. A studio is a special room within the station. It has microphones and other equipment for broadcasting.

A broadcaster can also work away from the studio in **remote,** or distant, locations such as baseball parks. Special wiring and broadcasting instruments make remote broadcasts possible.

A TV station engineer checks out studio equipment before a live broadcast begins

Students in broadcasting schools learn how to operate studio TV cameras

*This technician at a big-city TV station has a full-time job
repairing broadcast equipment*

ON THE AIR!

When broadcasters speak into microphones, they are "on the air." Their voices are sent through the air as signals from broadcasting stations. Electric instruments send the signals to radios and TVs with the help of huge transmitting towers and **satellites** in space.

Audiences with their sets tuned to the correct stations hear the broadcasters' words instantly.

An engineer in a TV studio control room oversees a giant switchboard

WHO CAN BE A BROADCASTER?

Broadcasting can be an exciting job. Broadcasters sometimes work with famous people and important events. A broadcaster's words can reach thousands, even millions, of listeners.

Many young people would like to be broadcasters. Most of those who will become broadcasters will read well, speak clearly and have pleasant speaking voices.

One voice on a microphone may reach thousands of people in homes, cars and workplaces

THE BROADCASTER'S EQUIPMENT

Broadcasts require special equipment. In TV stations especially, screens, knobs, dials, lights and switches seem to be everywhere. Radio stations have far fewer gadgets.

Broadcasters at large radio and TV stations don't handle much equipment themselves. They speak into microphones, and a TV broadcaster is likely to read from a **TelePrompTer** screen. The TelePrompTer displays the words that the broadcaster reads.

A TV station technician checks monitor screens in the video tape technical center

THE BROADCASTER'S HELPERS

Broadcasters at large radio and TV stations have several helpers. **Interns** are student assistants who are learning about broadcasting. **Engineers** operate equipment. **Producers** help plan programs and make sure they proceed smoothly. **Technicians** arrange and repair equipment.

Broadcasters also work with the station director, sales people who sell advertising, and computer operators.

A technician climbs into a jungle of studio lights in preparation for a TV broadcast

LEARNING TO BE A BROADCASTER

Most successful broadcasters took classes in speech, writing and broadcasting. Many colleges offer such classes. Some colleges offer on-the-job experience at their own radio stations.

Broadcasting schools also offer job training. Students learn how to use equipment, how broadcasts are made, and how to speak more clearly.

Intern jobs at radio and TV stations offer excellent on-the-job training, but they are difficult jobs to find.

Glossary

engineer (en gin EAR) — a person who manages various controls

intern (IN tern) — a student hired temporarily to gain on-the-job experience

microphone (MIKE ruh phone) — an instrument for transmitting or recording sound

producer (pro DO sir) — a person who plans and manages the production of a TV or radio program

remote (re MOTE) — somewhere far away or out-of-the-way

satellite (SAT el ite) — a human-made object that is rocketed into orbit and often used for communication

technician (tehk NISH un) — a person who operates or repairs various instruments

TelePrompTer (TEL uh prom ter) — a device that displays words for a TV broadcaster to read

INDEX